Handmade
Card & Thread
Greetings Cards

Polly Pinder

SEARCH PRESS

First published in Great Britain 2004

Search Press Limited
Wellwood, North Farm Road,
Tunbridge Wells, Kent TN2 3DR

ISBN 1 84448 005 4

If you have difficulty obtaining any of the equipment or materials mentioned in this book, please visit our website at **www.searchpress.com.**

Alternatively, you can write to the Publishers, at the address above, for a current list of stockists, including firms which operate a mail-order service.

Publishers' note
All the step-by-step photographs in this book feature the author, Polly Pinder, demonstrating how to make handmade greetings cards. No models have been used.

Printed in Spain by Elkar S. Coop., Bilbao 48012

ACKNOWLEDGEMENTS
I would like to thank Craft Basics of Gillygate, York, for providing many of the threads used in the making of projects in this book.
Many thanks also to Whispers™ for permission to use the butterfly rubber stamp that features in the card shown on pages 40 and 48.

Cover
Feathered Flower
Brightly coloured feather dusters are a useful purchase for the card maker, and more economic than buying packets of individual feathers. A thickly textured gold thread has been used for the flower centre and a delicate, finer one for the petals. The middle of the centre is a self-adhesive, flat-backed gemstone made from soft plastic. These are bought on a sheet containing a variety of shapes and colours.

Page 1
Flower Repeats
Repeating images with a slight variation in colour is always a good design ploy; and uneven numbers – three, five, or seven, are somehow more visually pleasing. The highly textured paper is made in India from recycled cotton and other natural materials.

Page 3
Moonlit Cat
Fine black wool with an intertwining multicoloured metallic thread was used for this cat. Regular card makers should try to keep a stock of second-hand papers and card – the moon and eyes were cut from the lid of a chocolate box.

Page 5
Spring Butterflies
There are numerous styles of craft stickers available to enhance your card and thread designs. Images which are texturally very different can be brought together by the use of colour. Here yellow and green have been taken from the stickers and used for the threaded butterfly.

Handmade
Card & Thread
Greetings Cards

*To my beloved brother and sister-in-law,
Simon and Harriette, for their unstinting
love and support, and to their beautiful
children, Alice and Dominic.*

Contents

Introduction

One of the lovely aspects of card and thread is that the structure of each threaded shape can look extremely complex, as if it must have taken hours of painstaking work to create, but once the simple technique has been mastered, stunning threaded shapes can be quickly and easily produced.

Some readers may remember a craft called 'pin and thread', in which rows of shiny-headed nails were banged into pieces of wood, then threads of string, wool, cotton, raffia or fine wire were wound round the nails to produce spectacular images. Card and thread is very similar. The principle is the same: the act of winding thread to create an image, but nails and pins are not required. Instead, notches, Vs or slits are cut into the card shape, then thread is wound round the shape and is caught and secured in the notches. A pattern is created, with the design governed by how many notches, Vs or slits are missed during the winding process. It sounds much more complicated than it is: once you get winding there'll be no stopping you, and the design possibilities are endless.

There are many beautiful papers and cards available to complement your card and thread designs: they come in all textures and shades and can be chosen from craft shops or picked up wherever you see them: I have used an office folder and a chocolate box lid whilst preparing cards for this book.

Striking new metallic threads are now available in a variety of plies and textures, and there are silky and satin threads in a multitude of colours, or multicoloured ones that vary in tone, all just waiting to be wound intriguingly into the shape of a flower, a cat or butterfly.

I have always believed that a beautifully handmade greetings card, created with patience and love, is equal to any expensive gift. It will always be treasured by the recipient. I hope that the step-by-step projects and the other cards shown in this book will generate enthusiasm and inspire readers to create many wonderful card and thread images.

Polly

Materials

Card and papers

The card used to make your greetings cards needs only to be stiff enough to stand up when folded in half and decorated with your card and thread artwork. The card used to make the shapes needs to be as rigid as possible so that pulling the threads across will not distort it. If your chosen card is not sturdy enough, it can always be backed by a piece of mount board.

There is a wonderful variety of cards and papers available today: from textured handmade papers to glossy or pearlescent card or self-adhesive foil – so be adventurous. Even old-fashioned wood chip wallpaper can look surprisingly effective: see the ginger cat on page 34. Highly textured papers made from cotton pulp make fascinating backgrounds: see the row of flowers on page 1 and the initialled heart on page 23. You can also decorate your own paper backgrounds: the black and white striped paper used for the abstract design on page 29 was produced on the computer, but lines carefully drawn with felt-tipped pen would be equally effective.

The thicker gold thread used here gives the card a wonderfully dramatic feel, with hot red, gold and the cool cream background combining to make a sumptuous gift for someone you love.

For these cards, a softer look is achieved by using pastel shades and non-metallic thread. For the long, pink card, the handmade tissue paper was stuck on using a glue stick. The tiny pearlescent hearts are often used to scatter on the tables at wedding feasts.

Opposite: For the little red card, the highly textured paper was stiff enough to make the actual greetings card. A piece of ordinary paper would need to be inserted to write the greeting.

The printing stamp for the heart-shaped card was made from a piece of polystyrene packing.

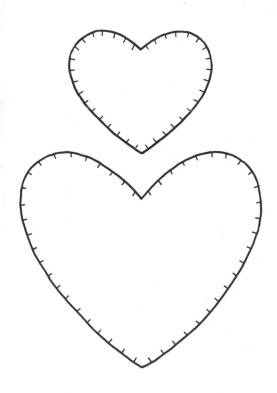

Templates for the threaded shapes on these cards

23

Metallic Abstract

Any abstract shape can be made to look stunning when lovely metallic threads are pulled across it. Here, one shape has been used twice, pointing in different directions. Although the card used is fairly thick, it is not rigid enough to withstand the threads pulling in so many directions across an asymmetrical shape. For this reason, mount board has been used as a backing to prevent the shapes from distorting.

You will need

Silver card blank,
100 x 210mm (4 x 8½in)

Navy card, 100 x 210mm
(4 x 8½in)

Mount board, 100 x 210mm
(4 x 8½in)

Fine, smooth metallic threads,
copper and gold

Fine, rough metallic
thread, silver

Tracing paper and HB pencil

White pencil and eraser

Sticky tape

Double-sided tape

Clear all-purpose glue

Scissors

Craft knife and cutting mat

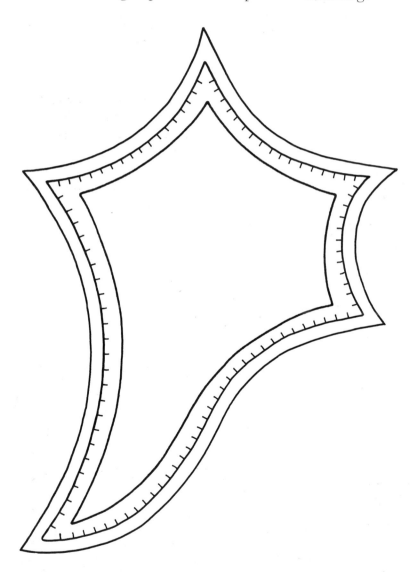

The templates for the Metallic Abstract card (the inner lines) and for the cards on page 29 (the outer line).

1. Trace the larger shape on to tracing paper. Turn over and scribble over the image with the white pencil. Lay the tracing on to the navy blue card and transfer the image by drawing over the lines with a sharp HB pencil. Repeat to make a second shape the same size.

2. Cut the card shapes out. Using your craft knife and cutting mat, cut small slits at each white pencil mark round the edges. When you have finished, rub off any remaining white pencil with an eraser.

3. Transfer the smaller shape twice on to mount board and cut the two shapes out. Attach them to the back of the navy shapes using double-sided tape.

Tip

When cutting a shape from mount board, use a craft knife and cutting mat rather than scissors, which are likely to distort the board.

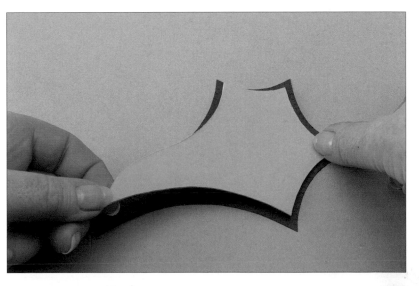

 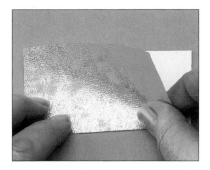 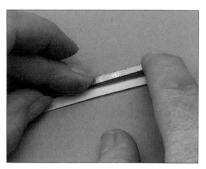

1. Trace the four separate wings and transfer them on to white card. Cut them out using the deckle-edged scissors to create the curved, serrated edge. Rub off any pencil marks.

2. Cut a piece 45 x 85mm (3¼ x 1¾in) from the remaining white card. Cover it with green self-adhesive foil. Turn it over and transfer the double wings on to the back. Cut them out using scissors.

3. Cut a strip of mount board 5 x 65mm (³⁄₈ x 2½in). Cover with the same self-adhesive foil, then round off each end with scissors, to make the butterfly's body.

4. Using three strands of embroidery thread, start winding the single wings. Attach the thread to the back using a piece of sticky tape and wind from the indent to the nearest notch. Work clockwise, catching every alternate notch, then go backwards catching all those that were missed. Repeat with the other three wings.

5. Secure the metallic thread to the back of a large wing. Catch the fifth notch (counting from the indent), and take the thread across to the twelfth notch (counting from the other side of the indent). Go back to the fifth and across to the thirteenth, fourteenth and fifteenth notches. Move on to the eighth notch and repeat, winding across to the sixteenth, seventeenth, eighteenth and nineteenth. Move on to the eleventh notch and across to twenty, twenty-one and twenty-two. Secure the thread and repeat with the other large wing.

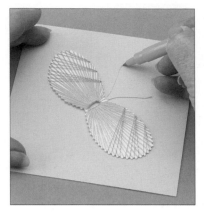

6. Secure the metallic thread to the back of a small wing. Catch the fifth notch and take the thread across to the eleventh, back up to the fifth and across to the twelfth, thirteenth and fourteenth. Secure at the back and repeat with the other wing.

7. Position the large wings diagonally across the card blank and secure them using all-purpose glue. Lightly trace the antennae, then draw over the lines with the felt-tipped pen.

8. Glue the small wings on to the foiled double wing base.

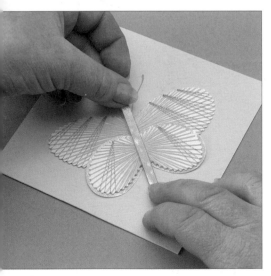

9. Glue the smaller wing base on to the larger wings. Run a trail of glue along the underside of the body and position it between the wings.

10. Punch out the dragonflies from the self-adhesive foil, peel off the backing and use a craft knife to pick them up and place them on the card.

This card with its subtle colours combined with glitter and shine, suggests the intricate beauty of the insect world. Craft punches are a wonderful addition to the card maker's toolbox. It would have taken forever to produce these little dragonflies by hand!

Above: A rubber-stamped image complements the card and thread design. Don't forget to protect your working surface when using a rubber stamp if the image goes beyond the edges of the greetings card. The decorative wing spots were cut with an office hole punch.
Opposite top: Crinkly silk thread is used here, the colours replicating those of the craft stickers. Colour coordination always helps to unify a design.
Bottom: This background is a beautiful random-lace paper which was stuck on to the greetings card. The butterfly body is a piece of card with two strings of tiny beads secured using double-sided tape.

Bubbly Fish

These two goldfish, swimming in a sea of bubbles, can be threaded very easily once the shapes have been cut and the little slits round the edges have been made. Each fish has a body and a separate tail. The bubbles are threaded and caught in slits in the top and bottom edges of the card. These threads are not wound round, but secured at the top and bottom of the reverse side and neatly covered by a piece of card.

You will need

Pale blue card blank,
100 x 210mm (4 x 8½in)

Darker blue card, 100mm
(4in) square

Two strips of pale blue card,
15 x 95mm (⅝ x 3¾in)

Small piece of bronze
self-adhesive card

Fine embroidery thread in
various shades of orange

Pale blue embroidery thread

Ninety tiny gold beads and
beading needle

Single hole punch

Double-sided tape

Sticky tape

Clear all-purpose glue

Tracing paper, HB pencil,
white pencil and eraser

Craft knife and cutting mat

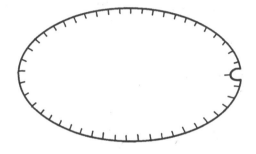

The templates for the Bubbly Fish card

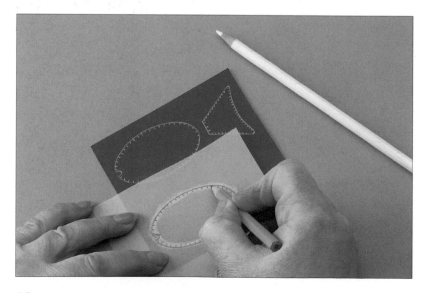

1. Trace the fish shapes. Turn the tracing paper over and scribble over the images with the white pencil. Lay the tracing right-side-up on the darker blue card and transfer the images by drawing over the lines with a sharp HB pencil. Repeat for the second fish.

42

2. Carefully cut out the card shapes and, using a craft knife and cutting mat, cut small slits at each pencil mark. Rub out any remaining white pencil using an eraser.

3. Secure the orange thread with sticky tape at the back of a fish body shape. Catch the thread through the slit in the mouth and take it to the twenty-fourth slit directly opposite. Take it back up behind, catch the second slit, then go over to the twenty-fifth and so on.

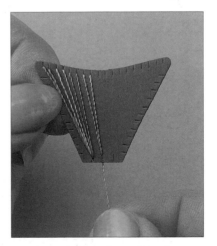

4. When the first round is complete, catch the slit fourth from the mouth, leave fifteen slits and catch the sixteenth. Go behind and up to the fifth, across to the seventeenth and so on. Secure at the back after the fourth slit on the other side of the mouth.

5. Secure the thread and hold the tail as shown. The tail has three slits at the narrow end. Start from the left-hand slit and wind to the six left-hand slits at the wider end, working left to right. Then wind from the middle slit to the six middle slits, and from the right-hand slit to the six right-hand slits.